The Tree House

KATHLEEN JAMIE was born in the west of Scotland in 1962. *The Tree House* won both the Forward Prize and the Scottish Book of the Year Award and *Mr and Mrs Scotland are Dead* was shortlisted for the 2003 International Griffin Prize. Kathleen Jamie's non-fiction books include the highly regarded *Findings* and *Sightlines*. She is Chair of Creative Writing at Stirling University, and lives with her family in Fife.

The Tree House

KATHLEEN JAMIE

PICADOR

First published 2004 by Picador
an imprint of Pan Macmillan, a division of Macmillan Publishers Limited
Pan Macmillan, 20 New Wharf Road, London N1 9RR
Basingstoke and Oxford
Associated companies throughout the world
www.panmacmillan.com

ISBN 978-0-330-43332-7

7 9 8 6

A CIP catalogue record for this book is available from
the British Library.

Typeset by Macmillan Design Department
Printed and bound by CPI Group (UK) Ltd, Croydon, CR0 4YY

Visit **www.picador.com** to read more about all our books
and to buy them. You will also find features, author interviews and
news of any author events, and you can sign up for e-newsletters
so that you're always first to hear about our new releases.

Acknowledgements

Acknowledgements are due to the editors of the following: *Chapman*, *Flora Poetica*, *London Review of Books*, the *New Yorker*, *Irish Pages*, *Irish Review*, *Irish Times*, *Poetry Review*, *Times Literary Supplement*, Watford Theatre.

Several of the poems have been broadcast on BBC Radio. 'The Glass-hulled Boat' was commissioned by Radio 3's Poetry Proms series. 'The Wishing Tree' was written for the King's Singers, and performed at the Proms 2002, to music by Joby Talbot. 'Hoard' was commissioned by Salisbury Festival and appeared in the anthology *Last Words*, edited by Don Paterson and Jo Shapcott.

David Constantine's translations of Hölderlin (Bloodaxe Books, 1990) formed the basis of the versions in Scots.

Special thanks are due to the Scottish Arts Council for the Creative Scotland award, which made this book possible.

But it is beautiful to unfold our souls
And our short lives

HÖLDERLIN

Contents

The Tree House

The Wishing Tree

I stand neither in the wilderness
nor fairyland

but in the fold
of a green hill

the tilt from one parish
into another.

To look at me
through a smirr of rain

is to taste the iron
in your own blood

because I hoard
the common currency

of longing: each wish
each secret assignation.

My limbs lift, scabbed
with greenish coins

I draw into my slow wood
fleur-de-lys, the enthroned Britannia.

Behind me, the land
reaches towards the Atlantic.

And though I'm poisoned
choking on the small change

of human hope,
daily beaten into me

look: I am still alive –
in fact, in bud.

Frogs

But for her green
palpitating throat, they lay
inert as a stone, the male
fastened like a package
to her back. They became,

as you looked, almost
beautiful, her back
mottled to leafy brown,
his marked with two stripes,
pale as over-wintered grass.

When he bucked, once,
neither so much as blinked;
their oval, gold-lined eyes
held to some bog-dull
imperative. The car

that would smear them
into one – belly
to belly, tongue thrust
utterly into soft brain –
approached and pressed on

Oh how we press on –
the car and passengers, the slow
creatures of this earth,
the woman by the verge
with her hands cupped.

Alder

Are you weary, alder tree,
in this, the age of rain?

From your branches
droop clots of lichen

like fairy lungs. All week,
squalls, tattered mists:

alder, who unfolded
before the receding glaciers

first one leaf then another,
won't you teach me

a way to live
on this damp ambiguous earth?

The rain showers
release from you a broken tune

but when the sun blinks, as it must,
how you'll sparkle –

like a fountain in a wood
of untold fountains.

Water Day

For four hours every eight days
our terraces' *acequias*
run with snow-melt,
sufficient for the almond
and orange trees, poppies,
irises, pimpernels.

And whether it's the water's
urgency or the beauty
of its governance, the way
it slakes the clay-
lined channels, its blithe
career through sluice gates;
or the fig tree
swelling over holding tanks
as water spills
through weedy gullets,
oracular and olive-green –

couldn't we make
heavy weather of it all?
Proof of remote
beneficent mountains; the mind's
release from silence, the boll
and eagre of sex, perhaps,
or poetry?

Or we might just follow
the custom hereabouts,
and rise at dawn on water day,
walk a mile in its company
as it falls, level
down to level, till it simply
quits the tenancy of our short lives,
and let it go.

The Fountain of the Lions

Gilded in Arabic
round its damp rim,
a praise-poem hymns
the *difficult, perfect*

system of hydraulics
by which rising water
branches into twelve,
each the tongue of a lion.

The marble dish
they bear on their backs
brims over, replenishes
and overbrims, as they stare

to every sorrowful
quarter of the world,
streams coursing endless
from their jaws.

The Cave of the Fish

It winds through sage,
cypresses, rock rose –
the drove road long

shared by goatherds
and fisherfolk. At noon
they'd retreat to a high cave,

seclude their wares
deep in its shade,
talk there, or doze.

Though some of them
had a whiff of the beast,
others a hint of brine,

the path below led home
for both, neither
more true nor more right.

Today I sit at the cave's
cool mouth, halfway
through my life.

For When the Grape-vine's Sap

(efter Hölderlin)

For when the grape-vine's sap
thon canny plant, seeks shedda,
an the grape swells
ablo a caller pend o leaves,
it gies smeddum tae men;
but tae lasses, sweetness
– an bees, steer't wi the speerit
o the sun, bedrucken
wi spring's braith
bummle efter it,
but when the sun beeks,
fey-like, they turn hame

          abune
            the aik reeshles

Before the Wind

If I'm to happen upon the hill
where cherries grow wild
it better be soon, or the yellow-
eyed birds will come squabbling,

claiming the fruit for their own.
Wild means stones barely
clothed in flesh, but that's rich
coming from me. A mouth

contains a cherry, a cherry
a stone, a stone
the flowering branch
I must find before the wind

scatters all trace of its blossom,
and the fruit comes, and yellow-eyed birds.

Speirin

Binna feart, hinny,
yin day we'll gang thegither
tae thae stourie
blaebellwids,
and loss wirsels –

see, I'd raither
whummel a single oor
intae the blae o thae wee flo'ers
than live fur a' eternity
in some cauld hivvin.

Wheest, nou, till I spier o ye
will ye haud wi me?

Landfall

When we walk at the coast
and notice, above the sea,
a single ragged swallow
veering towards the earth-
and blossom-scented breeze,
can we allow ourselves to fail

The Swallows' Nest

(for P. B.)

Shutters, broken,
firewood, a rake, a wrought-
iron bed, the torch-lit
rafters of the lumber-room,
you showing me

one bird tucked in a home-
made bracket of spittle
and earth, while its mate slept
perched on the rim, at an angle
exact as a raised latch.

The Bower

Neither born nor gifted
crafted nor bequeathed
this forest dwelling's little
but a warp or tease

in the pliant light
trees soften and confine.
Though it's nothing
but an attitude of mind

mere breath rising in staves,
the winds assail
its right to exist, this anchorage
or musical box, veiled

and listing deep
in the entailed estate,
sure only of its need
to annunciate.

But when song, cast
from such frail enclaves
meets the forest's edge,
it returns in waves

Swallows

I wish my whole battened
heart were a property
like this, with swallows
in every room – so at ease

they twitter and preen
from the picture frames
like an audience in the gods
before an opera

and in the mornings
wheel above my bed
in a mockery of pity
before winging it

up the stairwell
to stream out into light

The Blue Boat

How late the daylight edges
toward the northern night
as though journeying
in a blue boat, gilded in mussel shell

with, slung from its mast, a lantern
like our old idea of the soul

Gloaming

We are flying, this summer's night, toward a brink, a wire-thin
rim of light. It swells as we descend, then illuminates the land
enough to let us name, by hill or river mouth, each township below.
This is the North, where people, the world perhaps likes to imagine,
hold a fish in one hand, in the other a candle.
I could settle for that. The plane shudders, then rolls to a standstill
at the far end of the runway. It's not day, this light we've entered,
but day is present at the negotiation. The sky's the still
pale grey of a heron, attending the tide-pools of the shore.

The Glass-hulled Boat

First come the jellyfish:
mauve-fringed, luminous bowls
like lost internal organs,
pulsing and slow.

Then in the green gloom
swaying sideways and back
like half-forgotten ancestors
– columns of bladderwrack.

It's as though we're stalled in a taxi
in an ill-lit, odd
little town, at closing time,
when everyone's maudlin

and really, ought just to *go
home*, you sorry inclining
pillars of wrack, you lone,
vaguely uterine jellyfish

– whom I almost envy:
spun out, when our engines churn,
on some sudden new trajectory,
fuddled, but unperturbed.

White-sided Dolphins

When there was no doubt,
no mistaking for water-glint
their dorsal fins'
urgent cut and dive

we grabbed cameras, threw ourselves
flat on the fore-deck. Then,
just for a short time
we travelled as one

loose formation: the muscular
wingers, mothers-with-young,
old scarred outriders
all breached alongside,

took it in turn
to swoon up through our pressure-wave,
careen and appraise us
with a speculative eye

till they'd seen enough,
when true to their own
inner oceanic maps, the animals
veered off from us, north by northwest.

Basking Shark

When I came to the cliff-edge
and lay down, all beneath
was space, then green-
tinted sea, so clear
it revealed, level below level,
not void, but a living creature.

Behind me peat moor
careered inland. I gripped
sweet rock – but it was only
resting, berthed as though
drawn by the cliff's
peculiar backwash,

precisely that its ore-
heavy body and head –
the tail fin measuring back,
forth, like a haunted door –
could come to sense the absolute
limits of its realm.

While it hung, steady
as an anvil but for the fins'
corrective rippling – dull,
dark and buoyed like a heart
that goes on living
through a long grief

what could one do but watch?
The sea heaved; fulmars
slid by on static wings;
the shark – not ready yet
to re-enter the ocean
travel there, peaceable and dumb –

waited, and was watched;
till it all became
unbearable, whereupon the wind
in its mercy breathed again
and far below the surface
glittered, and broke up.

The Whale-watcher

And when at last the road
gives out, I'll walk –
harsh grass, sea-maws,
lichen-crusted bedrock –

and hole up the cold
summer in some battered
caravan, quartering
the brittle waves

till my eyes evaporate
and I'm willing again
to deal myself in:
having watched them

breach, breathe, and dive
far out in the glare,
like stitches sewn in a rent
almost beyond repair.

Selchs

Daur we, ma jo,
dae lik thae selchs, sae
inglamourt bi the saumon-rin

thae dinnae tak wit
til thur somewhaur wanchancy –
caller-watter, taintit wi peat?

The Buddleia

When I pause to consider
a god, or creation unfolding
in front of my eyes –
is this my lot? Always
brought back to the same
grove of statues in ill-
fitting clothes: my suddenly
elderly parents, their broken-down
Hoover; or my quarrelling kids?

Come evening, it's almost too late
to walk in the garden, and try,
once again, to retire the masculine
God of my youth
by evoking instead the divine
in the lupins, or foxgloves, or self-
seeded buddleia,
whose heavy horns flush as they
open to flower, and draw
these bumbling, well-meaning bees
which remind me again,
of my father . . . whom, Christ,
I've forgotten to call.

Hame

(efter Hölderlin)

Wha's tae ken
if whiles Ah dauner
yur back-braes, O Yird
and pu wild berries
tae slocken ma luve fur ye
– here whaur jags o roses
and gean-trees
pit oot thur sweet air,
aside the birks, at noon,

when, in the yella glebe
grouin corn reeshles,
and the ickers nod, like at hairst,
– but nou, ablo the aiks' lift,
whaur ah wunner an spier
heivenward, yonner
weel-kent bell jows
gowden notes,
at the oor the birds wauken
ance mair. An a's weel.

The Orchard

Here is the late half-land
where the underworld,
the moon-shadow of an apple tree

is a darkness, like the earth
we're called from –
silent but for a hush

like heavy skirts;
women, perhaps, passing
on the far side of a wall

whom we may call
our history; or a vole,
some creature of the dusk

when the arms of the slender
garden plum trees suddenly
turn muscular, and deepest blue.

Pipistrelles

In the centre of the sheep-field
a stand of Douglas firs
hold between them, tenderly,
a tall enclosure like a vase.

How could we have missed it
before today – never have seen
this clear, translucent vessel
tinted like citrine?

What we noticed were pipistrelles:
cinder-like, friable, flickering
the place hained by trees
till the air seemed to quicken

and the bats were a single
edgy intelligence, testing their idea
for a new form
which unfolded and cohered

before our eyes. The world's
mind is such interstices;
cells charging with light of day –
is that what they were telling us?

But they vanished, suddenly,
before we'd understood,
and the trees grew in a circle,
elegant and mute.

Daisies

We are flowers of the common
sward, that much we understand.
Of everything else
we're innocent. No Creator
laid down such terms
for our pleasant lives,
– it's just our nature,
were we not so,
we wouldn't be daisies, closing
our lashes at the first
suggestion of Venus. By then,
we're near exhausted. Evening
means sleep, and surely it's better
to renew ourselves than die
of all that openness?
But die we will, innocent
or no, of how night
spills above our garden,
twins glittering there
for each of us; die
never knowing what we miss.

Rhododendrons

It wasn't sand martins
hunting insects in the updraught,
or the sudden scent of bog myrtle

that made me pause, lean
across the parapet,
but a handful of purple baubles

reflected below the water's surface
as comfortable and motionless
as a family in their living room

watching TV. What was it,
I'd have asked, to exist
so bright and fateless

while time coursed
through our every atom
over its bed of stones – ?

But darkness was weighing
the flowers and birds' backs,
and already my friends had moved on.

Water Lilies

Late summer: the white
flowers are blown,
but furled leaf-cones

persist in rising
through the peat-stained
lochan's shallows

till they reach the open
border where water
becomes air, and there

unfold: pale green
almost heart shapes,
almost upturned hands.

Stane-raw

Xanthoria parietina

Your yellowish mark
of salt on rock's
found miles inland
on gravestones, chimneys,
any limit of the sea's
breath. And though we know
your subtle bond
endures a lifetime,
what we desire
is your leaden blue dye.
Our kisses are fleet, invisible;
should we wish to
keep or carry one, we must
transmute it to a bruise-
coloured tattoo, hidden
beneath our clothing, like this
indelible dog rose
inked on my shoulder,
the finch on my inner thigh.

Hoard

What kind of figure did he cut
huddled in the dusk, gut wound
packed with sphagnum,
as he sank into the bog
his offering of weaponry,
blades courteously broken,
his killed cherished swords?

Reliquary

The land we inhabit opens to reveal
the stain of ancient settlements,
plague pits where we'd lay
our fibre-optic cables;

but witness these brittle August
bluebells casting seed,
like tiny hearts in caskets
tossed onto a battle ground.

Moult

At a certain time of year
come floating shorewards
innumerable seabirds'
primaries and coverts.

Though they're dead things
washed up on the sand
each carries a part
– a black tip, say, to the vane –

of the pattern the outstretched
wing displays. What
can one frayed feather
tell of that design,

or the covenant they undertake,
wind and kittiwake?

Flight of Birds

From our gardens the mavis is melted away,
she is gravel; waders veer overhead
crying *whither? whither?* and the poor duck
flusters at the roadside with her clipped wings.

– Suppose as a last ditch, we gathered
empty-handed at the town's edge and called
each bird by name, might we yet prevail
upon wren, water rail, tiny anointed goldcrest

to remain within our sentience in this,
the only world? There is no Paradise,
we've humiliated living creatures,
bidding them lie down with one another

through our own unease – if *they* greet dawn
by singing of a better place, can we complain?
Below a hill, a cave mouth is closing now
even as the yellow-taloned merlin tilts inside.

The Falcon

To the disused quarry
behind our town the single
peregrine fledged there this May
returns and returns. His father
and mother flown, he must be master
already, of a falcon's skills –
to judge the greenwood
so exquisitely his wing tips
graze not a leaf; to ascend
almost out of the world,
then stoop, snapping a pigeon's neck;
he's discovered
or tenderly been shown
every sheltering niche, for hitherto
God's tempered the wind
to the unmeek hawk, but soon
will come winter. It's here,
his native familiar,
he seeks reassurance,
stepping out of empty air
to a rock ledge so weathered now
it could be natural.
He preens, then closes
his constant eyes. In retreat
he becomes most visible.

The Tree House

Hands on a low limb, I braced,
swung my feet loose, hoisted higher,
heard the town clock toll, a car
breenge home from a club
as I stooped inside. Here

I was unseeable. A bletted fruit
hung through tangled branches
just out of reach. Over house roofs:
sullen hills, the firth drained
down to sandbanks: the *Reckit Lady*, the *Shair as Daith*.

I lay to sleep,
beside me neither man
nor child, but a lichened branch
wound through the wooden chamber,
pulling it close; a complicity

like our own, when arm in arm
on the city street, we bemoan
our families, our difficult
chthonic anchorage
in the apple-sweetened earth,

without whom we might have lived
the long ebb of our mid-decades
alone in sheds and attic rooms,
awake in the moonlit souterrains
of our own minds; without whom

we might have lived
a hundred other lives,
like taxis strangers hail and hire,
that turn abruptly on the gleaming setts
and head for elsewhere.

Suppose just for the hell of it
we flagged one – what direction would we give?
Would we still be driven here,
our small-town Ithacas, our settlements
hitched tight beside the river

where we're best played out
in gardens of dockens
and lady's mantle, kids' bikes
stranded on the grass;
where we've knocked together

of planks and packing chests
a dwelling of sorts; a gall
we've asked the tree to carry
of its own dead, and every spring
to drape in leaf and blossom, like a pall.

The Cupboard

As for this muckle
wooden cupboard carted hither
years ago, from some disused
branch-line station, the other
side of the hill, that takes up
more room than the rest of us
put together, like a dour
homesick whale, or mute sarcophagus –

why is it at *my* place?
And how did it sidle
through the racked,
too-narrow door, to hunker
below these sagging rafters,
no doubt for evermore?

The Creel

The world began with a woman,
shawl-happed, stooped under a creel,
whose slow step you recognize
from troubled dreams. You feel

obliged to help bear her burden
from hill or kelp-strewn shore,
but she passes by unseeing
thirled to her private chore.

It's not sea birds or peat she's carrying,
not fleece, nor the herring bright
but her fear that if ever she put it down
the world would go out like a light.

The Brooch

All I have is small enough
to be held in one hand –
an agate brooch. It's pierced

like an implement or tool,
perhaps a loom weight.
The agates are brindled,

grey, like carded wool,
or the rings inside a cup, drained,
set to be washed on a table.

Of the woman who pinned it
to her plain coat, only this remains:
her gift, my heirloom, stones.

The Puddle

A week's worth of rain
gathers in swing-parks;
pools in hollow
low-lying fields

give the come-hither
to oystercatchers; curlews
insert like thermometers
their elegant bills.

What is it to lie so
level with the world,
to encourage the eye-
for-the-main-chance

black-headed gulls,
goal-posts, willows,
purple-bellied clouds
to inhabit us, briefly

upside down?
Is it written that we
with some life left,
must stake our souls

upright within us
as the grey-hackled heron
by a pond's rim,
ever forbidding

the setting winter sun
to scald us beautifully
ruby and carnelian?
Flooded fields, all pulling

the same lustrous trick,
that flush in the world's light
as though with sudden love –
how should we live?

The Dipper

It was winter, near freezing,
I'd walked through a forest of firs
when I saw issue out of the waterfall
a solitary bird.

It lit on a damp rock,
and, as water swept stupidly on,
wrung from its own throat
supple, undammable song.

It isn't mine to give.
I can't coax this bird to my hand
that knows the depth of the river
yet sings of it on land.